# FIGHT AGAINST ENEMY - 2

MR VIVEK KUMAR PANDEY
SHAMBHUNATH

# Contents

# CHAPTER ONE

## *What is Surgical Strike or Operation?*

The **Surgical Strike or Surgical Operation** is a military attack which is intended to damage only a legitimate military target, with no or minimal collateral damage to surrounding structures, vehicles, buildings, or the general public infrastructure and utilities. This kind of operation or strike requires intense coordination among the government, intelligence agencies and the security forces for the success. These are quick and effective strike or operation and also the reinforcement of commandos are kept on standby for any eventuality.

Top amazing facts about RAW

## *How Surgical Strike or Operation is followed up?*

This is an act of the Armed Forces that can be followed up through raiding air, airdropping or ground strike by the team of **Special Operations (ops) Forces.** These **special-operations force** trained enough to conduct sabotage, reconnaissance, subversive and other special operations on the territory of foreign countries during early morning hours as an **'element of surprise''.**

CH 2 OPERATION VIJAY

# Annexation of Goa

(Redirected from <u>Operation Vijay (1961)</u>)

*"Invasion of Goa" redirects here. For the conquest by Portugal in 1510, see <u>Portuguese conquest of Goa</u>.*

*"Operation Vijay (1961)" redirects here. For the 1999 Indian operation, see <u>Kargil War</u>.*

*See also: <u>Integration of Dadra and Nagar Haveli</u>*

**Annexation of Goa**

**Date**

18–19 December 1961

**Location**

vasco da gama

- <u>Goa, Daman and Diu</u>, <u>Portuguese India</u>
- Surrounding sea and airspace

**Result**

- Indian victory

Incorporation of the territories of Goa, Daman and Diu into the Republic of India

**Strength**

45,000 infantry

1 light aircraft carrier

2 cruisers

1 destroyer

8 frigates

4 minesweepers

20 <u>Canberra</u>medium bombers

6 <u>Vampire</u>fighters

6 Toofanifighter-bombers
6 Huntermulti-role aircraft
4 Mystèrefighter-bombers
   3,995 soldiers
200 sailors
1 frigate
3 patrol boats

**Casualties and losses**

   22 killed[1]

- 30 killed[2]
- 57 wounded[2]
- 1 frigate disabled[2][3]
- 4,668 captured[4]

   [a]Governor-General.

show

- v
- t
- e

## Portuguese colonial campaigns

The **Annexation of Goa**was the process in which the Republic of Indiaannexed the former Portuguese Indianterritories of Goa, Daman and Diu, starting with the armed action carried out by the Indian Armed Forcesin December 1961. In India, this action is referred as the "**Liberation of Goa**". In Portugal, it is referred to as the "**Invasion of Goa**". Following the end of Portuguese rule in 1961, Goa was placed under military administration headed by Kunhiraman Palat Candethas Lieutenant Governor.[5]On 8 June 1962, military rule was replaced by civilian government when the Lieutenant Governor nominated an informal Consultative Councilof 29 nominated members to assist him in the administration of the territory.[6]

The "armed action" was code named **Operation Vijay**(meaning "Victory") by the Indian Armed Forces. It involved air, sea and land strikes for over 36 hours, and was a decisive victory for India, ending 451 years of rule by Portugal over its remaining exclaves in India. The engagement lasted two days, and twenty-two Indians and thirty Portuguese were killed in the fighting.[2]The brief conflict drew a mixture of worldwide praise and condemnation. In India, the action was seen as a liberation of historically Indian territory, while Portugal viewed it as an aggression against its national soil and citizens.

# *Contents*

## Background[edit]

After India's independence from the British Empirein August 1947, Portugal continued to hold a handful of exclaveson the Indian subcontinent—the districts of Goa, Daman and Diuand Dadra and Nagar Haveli—collectively known as the *Estado da Índia*. Goa, Daman and Diu covered an area of around 1,540 square miles (4,000 km²) and held a population of 637,591.[7]The Goan diasporawas estimated at 175,000 (about 100,000 within the Indian Union, mainly in Bombay).[8]Religious distribution was 61% Hindu, 36.7% Christian (mostly Catholic) and 2.2% Muslim.[8]The economy was primarily based on agriculture, although the 1940s and 1950s saw a boom in mining—principally iron oreand some manganese.[8]

## *Local resistance to Portuguese rule*

*Main article: Goa Liberation Movement*

Resistance to Portuguese rule in Goa in the 20th century was pioneered by Tristão de Bragança Cunha, a French-educated Goan engineer who founded the Goa Congress Committee in Portuguese India in 1928. Cunha released a booklet called 'Four hundred years of Foreign Rule', and a pamphlet, 'Denationalisation of Goa', intended to sensitise Goans to the oppression of Portuguese rule. Messages of solidarity were received by the Goa Congress Committee from leading figures in the Indian independence movement including Rajendra Prasad, Jawaharlal Nehruand Subhas Chandra Bose. On 12 October 1938, Cunha with other members of the Goa Congress Committee met Subhas Chandra Bose, the President of the Indian National Congress, and on his advice, opened a Branch Office of the Goa Congress Committee at 21, Dalal Street, Bombay. The Goa Congress was also made affiliate to the Indian National Congress and Cunha was selected its first President.[9]

In June 1946, Ram Manohar Lohia, an Indian Socialist leader, entered Goa on a visit to his friend, Julião Menezes, a nationalist leader, who had founded the Gomantak Praja Mandal in Bombay and edited the weekly newspaper

*Gomantak.* Cunha and other leaders were also with him.[9]Ram Manohar Lohiaadvocated the use of non-violent Gandhiantechniques to oppose the government.[10]On 18 June 1946, the Portuguese government disrupted a protest against the suspension of civil liberties in Panaji(then spelt 'Panjim') organised by Lohia, Cunha and others including Purushottam Kakodkar and Laxmikant Bhembre in defiance of a ban on public gatherings, and arrested them.[11][12]There were intermittent mass demonstrations from June to November.

In addition to non-violent protests, armed groups such as the Azad Gomantak Dal (The Free Goa Party) and the United Front of Goans conducted violent attacks aimed at weakening Portuguese rule in Goa.[13]The Indian governmentsupported the establishment of armed groups like the Azad Gomantak Dal, giving them full financial, logistic and armament support. The armed groups acted from bases situated in Indian territory and under cover of Indian police forces. The Indian government—through these armed groups—attempted to destroy economic targets, telegraph and telephone lines, road, water and rail transport, in order to impede economic activity and create conditions for a general uprising of the population.[14]A Portuguese army officer stationed with the army in Goa, Captain Carlos Azaredo, stated in 2001 in the Portuguese newspaper *Expresso*: "To the contrary to what is being said, the most evolved guerilla warfare which our Armed Forces encountered was in Goa. I know what I'm talking about, because I also fought in Angola and in Guiné. In 1961 alone, until December, around 80 policemen died. The major part of the terrorists of Azad Gomantak Dal were not Goans. Many had fought in the British Army, under General Montgomery, against the Germans."[15]

## *Diplomatic efforts to resolve Goa dispute*

*Main article: India–Portugal relations*

Goa, Western India

On 27 February 1950, the Government of India asked the Portuguese government to open negotiations about the future of Portuguese colonies in India.[16]Portugal asserted that its territory on the Indian subcontinent was not a colony but part of metropolitan Portugal and hence its transfer was non-negotiable, and that India had no rights to this territory because the Republic of India did not exist at the time when Goa came under Portuguese rule.[17]When the Portuguese government refused to respond to subsequent aide-mémoires in this regard, the Indian government, on 11 June 1953, withdrew its diplomatic mission from Lisbon.[18]

By 1954, the Republic of India instituted visa restrictions on travel from Goa to India which paralysed transport between Goa and other exclaves like Daman, Diu, Dadra and Nagar Haveli.[16]Meanwhile, the Indian Union of Dockers had, in 1954, instituted a boycott on shipping to Portuguese India.[19]Between 22 July and 2 August 1954, armed activists attacked and forced the surrender of Portuguese forces stationed in Dadra and Nagar Haveli.[20]

On 15 August 1955, 3000–5000 unarmed Indian activists[21]attempted to enter Goa at six locations and were violently repulsed by Portuguese police officers, resulting in the deaths of between 21[22]and 30[23]people.[24]The news of the massacre built public opinion in India against the presence of the Portuguese in Goa.[25]On 1 September 1955, India shut its consul office in Goa.[26]

In 1956, the Portuguese ambassador to France, Marcello Mathias, along with Portuguese Prime Minister António de Oliveira Salazar, argued in favour of a referendum in Goa to determine its future. This proposal was however rejected by the Ministers for Defence and Foreign Affairs. The demand for a referendum was repeated by presidential candidate General Humberto Delgadoin 1957.[16]

Prime Minister Salazar, alarmed by India's hinted threats at armed action against Portugal's presence in Goa, first asked the United Kingdom to mediate, then protested through Braziland eventually asked the United Nations Security Councilto intervene.[27]Mexicooffered the Indian government its influence in Latin America to bring pressure on the Portuguese to relieve tensions.[28]Meanwhile, Krishna Menon, India's defence minister and head of India's UN delegation, stated in no uncertain terms that India had not "abjured the use of force" in Goa.[27]The US ambassador to India, John Kenneth Galbraith, requested the Indian government on several occasions to resolve the issue peacefully through mediation and consensus rather than armed conflict.[29][30]

On 24 November 1961, *Sabarmati*, a passenger boat passing between the Portuguese-held island of Anjidivand the Indian port of Kochi, was fired upon by Portuguese ground troops, resulting in the death of a passenger and injuries to the chief engineer. The action was precipitated by Portuguese fears that the boat carried a military landing partyintent on storming the island.[31]The incidents lent themselves to fostering widespread public support in India for military action in Goa.

Eventually, on 10 December, nine days prior to the "armed action (code named Operation Vijay)", Nehru stated to the press: "Continuance of Goa under Portuguese rule is an impossibility".[27]The American response was to warn India that if and when India's armed action in Goa was brought to the UN security council, it could expect no support from the US delegation.[32]

## Annexation of Dadra and Nagar Haveli

This section **does not citeany sources**. Please help improve this sectionby adding citations to reliable sources. Unsourced material may be challenged and removed. *(December 2017) (Learn how and when to remove this template message)*

*Main article: Indian annexation of Dadra and Nagar Haveli*

The hostilities between India and Portugal started seven years before the annexation of Goa, when Dadra and Nagar Haveliwere invaded and occupied by pro-Indian forces with the support of the Indian authorities.

Dadraand Nagar Haveliwere two Portuguese landlocked exclaves of the Daman district, totally surrounded by Indian territory. The connection between the exclaves and the coastal territory of Daman had to be made by crossing about 20 kilometres (12 mi) of Indian territory. Dadra and Nagar Haveli did not have any Portuguese military garrison, but only police forces.

The Indian government started to develop isolation actions against Dadra and Nagar Haveli already in 1952, including the creation of impediments to the transit of persons and goods between the two landlocked enclaves and Daman. In July 1954, pro-Indian forces, including members of organisations like the United Front of Goans, the National Movement Liberation Organisation, the Rashtriya Swayamsevak Sanghand the Azad Gomantak Dal, with the support of Indian Police forces, began to launch assaults against Dadra and Nagar Haveli. On the night of 22 July, UFG forces stormed the small Dadra police station, killing Police Sergeant Aniceto do Rosário and Constable António Fernandes, who resisted the attack. On 28 July, RSS forces took Naroli police station.

Meanwhile, the Portuguese authorities asked the Indian Government for permission to cross the Indian territory with reinforcements to Dadra and Nagar Haveli, but no permission was given. Surrounded and prevented from receiving reinforcements by the Indian authorities, the Portuguese Administrator and police forces in Nagar Haveli eventually surrendered to the Indian police forces on 11 August 1954. Portugal appealed to the International Court of Justice, which, in a decision dated 12 April 1960,[33]stated that Portugal had sovereign rights over the territories of Dadra and Nagar Haveli but India had the right to deny passage to armed personnel of Portugal over Indian territories. Therefore, the Portuguese authorities could not legally pass through Indian territory.

## Events preceding the hostilities

## Indian military build-up

On receiving the go-ahead for military action and a mandate for the capture of all occupied territories for the Indian government, Lieutenant-General Chaudhari of India's Southern Army fielded the 17th Infantry Divisionand the 50th Parachute Brigadecommanded by Major-General K. P. Candeth. The assault on the enclave of Daman was assigned to the 1st battalion of the Maratha

Light Infantrywhile the operations in Diu were assigned to the 20th battalion of the Rajput Regimentand the 5th battalion of the Madras Regiment.[34]

Meanwhile, the Commander-in-Chief of India's Western Air Command, Air Vice Marshal Erlic Pinto, was appointed as the commander of all air resources assigned to the operations in Goa. Air resources for the assault on Goa were concentrated in the bases at Puneand Sambra(Belgaum).[34]The mandate handed to Pinto by the Indian Air Command was listed out as follows:

1. The destruction of Goa's lone airfield in Dabolim, without causing damage to the terminal building and other airport facilities.
2. Destruction of the wireless station at Bambolim, Goa.
3. Denial of airfields at Daman and Diu, which were, however, not to be attacked without prior permission.
4. Support to advancing ground troops.

The Indian Navydeployed two warships—the INS Rajput, an 'R' Class destroyer, and INS Kirpan, a Blackwood classanti-submarine frigate—off the coast of Goa. The actual attack on Goa was delegated to four task groups: a Surface Action Group comprising five ships: Mysore, Trishul, Betwa, Beasand Cauvery; a Carrier Group of five ships: Delhi, Kuthar, Kirpan, Khukriand Rajput centred on the light aircraft carrier Vikrant; a Mine Sweeping Group consisting of mine sweepers including Karwar, Kakinada, Cannonoreand Bimilipatan, and a Support Group which consisted of Dharini.[35]

## *Portuguese mandate*

In March 1960, <u>Portuguese Defence Minister</u>General <u>Júlio Botelho Moniz</u>told Prime Minister Salazar that a sustained Portuguese campaign against decolonisation would create for the army "a suicide mission in which we could not succeed". His opinion was shared by Army Minister Colonel <u>Afonso Magalhães de Almeida Fernandes</u>, by the Army under secretary of State Lieutenant-Colonel <u>Francisco da Costa Gomes</u>and by other top officers.[36]

Ignoring this advice, Salazar sent a message to Governor General <u>Manuel António Vassalo e Silva</u>in Goa on 14 December, in which he ordered the Portuguese forces in Goa to fight to the last man: "Do not expect the possibility of truce or of Portuguese prisoners, as there will be no surrender rendered because I feel that our soldiers and sailors can be either victorious or dead."[37]Salazar asked Vassalo e Silva to hold out for at least eight days, within which time he hoped to gather international support against the Indian invasion. Vassalo e Silva disobeyed Salazar to avoid the unnecessary loss of human lives and surrendered the following day after the Indian invasion.[37]

## *Portuguese military preparations*

Portuguese military preparations began in earnest in 1954, following the Indian economic blockade, the beginning of the anti-Portuguese attacks in Goa and the annexation of Dadra and Nagar Haveli. Three light infantry battalions (one each sent from Portugal, Angola and Mozambique) and support units were transported to Goa, reinforcing a locally raised battalion and increasing the Portuguese military presence there from almost nothing to 12,000 men.[15]Other sources state that, at the end of 1955, Portuguese forces in India represented a total of around

8,000 men (Europeans, Africans and Indians), including 7,000 in the land forces, 250 in the naval forces, 600 in the police and 250 in the Fiscal Guard, split between the districts of Goa, Daman and Diu.[38]Following the annexation of Dadra and Nagar Haveli, the Portuguese authorities markedly strengthened the garrison of Portuguese India, with units and personnel sent from the Metropoleand from the Portuguese African provinces of Angolaand Mozambique.

The Portuguese forces were organised as the Armed Forces of the State of India (FAEI, *Forças Armadas do Estado da Índia*), under a unified command headed by General Paulo Bénard Guedes, who combined the civil role of Governor-General with the military role of Commander-in-Chief. Guedes ended his commission in 1958, with General Vassalo e Silva being appointed to replace him in both the civil and military roles.[38]

The Portuguese government and military commands were, however, well aware that even with this effort to strengthen the garrison of Goa, the Portuguese forces would never be sufficient to face a conventional attack from the overwhelmingly stronger Indian Armed Forces. The Portuguese government hoped however to politically deter the Indian government from attempting a military aggression through the showing of a strong will to fight and to sacrifice to defend Goa.[38]

In 1960, during an inspection visit to Portuguese India and referring to a predictable start of guerrilla activities in Angola, the Under Secretary of State of the Army, Francisco da Costa Gomes, stated the necessity to reinforce the Portuguese military presence in that African territory, partly at the expense of the military presence in Goa, where the then existing 7,500 men were too many just to deal with anti-Portuguese actions, and too few to face an Indian invasion, which, if it were to occur, would have to be handled by other means. This led to the Portuguese forces in India suffering a sharp reduction to about 3,300 soldiers.[38]

Faced with this reduced force strength, the strategy employed to defend Goa against an Indian invasion was based on the *Plano Sentinela* (Sentinel Plan), which divided the territory into four defence sectors (North, Center, South and Mormugão), and the *Plano de Barragens* (Barrage Plan), which envisaged the demolition of all bridges to delay the invading army, as well as the mining of approach roads and beaches. Defence units were organised as four battlegroups(*agrupamentos*), with one assigned to each sector and tasked with slowing the progress of an invading force. Then-Captain Carlos Azaredo, who was stationed in Goa at the time of hostilities, described the Plano Sentinela in the Portuguese newspaper *Expresso* on 8 December 2001 as "a totally unrealistic and unachievable plan, which was quite incomplete. It was based on exchange of ground with time. But, for this purpose, portable communication equipment was necessary."[15]The plans to mine roads and beaches were also unviable because of a desperate shortage of mines.[39]

### Navy

The naval component of the FAEI were the Naval Forces of the State of India (FNEI, *Forças Navais do Estado da Índia*), headed by the Naval Commander of Goa, Commodore Raúl Viegas Ventura. The only significant Portuguese Navywarship present in Goa at the time of invasion was the sloopNRP *Afonso de Albuquerque*.[40]It was armed with four 120 mm guns capable of two shots per minute, and four automatic rapid-firing guns. In addition to the sloop, the Portuguese Naval Forces had three light patrol boats(*lanchas de fiscalização*), each armed with a 20 mm Oerlikon gun, one based in each of Goa, Daman and Diu. There were also five merchant marineships in Goa.[41]An attempt by Portugal to send naval warships to Goa to reinforce its marine defences was foiled when President Nasserof Egyptdenied the ships access to the Suez Canal.[42][43][44]

### Ground forces[edit]

Portuguese ground defences were organised as the Land Forces of the State of India (FTEI, *Forças Terrestres do Estado da Índia*), under the Portuguese Army's Independent Territorial Command of India, headed by Brigadier António José Martins Leitão. At the time of the invasion, they consisted of a total of 3,995 men, including 810 native (*Indo-Portugueses* – Indo-Portuguese) soldiers, many of whom had little military training and were utilised primarily for security and anti-extremist operations. These forces were divided amongst the three Portuguese enclaves in India.[38]The Portuguese Army units in Goa included four motorised reconnaissance squadrons, eight rifle companies (*caçadores*), two artillery batteries and an engineer detachment. In addition to the military forces, the Portuguese defences counted on the civil internal security forcesof Portuguese India. These included the State of India Police(PEI, *Polícia do Estado da Índia*), a general police corps modelled after the Portuguese Public Security Police; the Fiscal Guard (*Guarda Fiscal*), responsible for Customsenforcement and border protection; and the Rural Guard (*Guarda Rural*), game wardens. In 1958, as an emergency measure, the Portuguese government gave provisional military status to the PEI and the Fiscal Guard, placing them under the command of the FAEI. The security forces were also divided amongst the three districts and were mostly made up of Indo-Portuguese policemen and guards. Different sources indicate between 900 and 1400 men as the total effective strength of these forces at the time of the invasion.[38]

### Air defence

The Portuguese Air Force did not have any presence in Portuguese India, with the exception of a single officer with the role of air adviser in the office of the Commander-in-Chief.[38]

On 16 December, the Portuguese Air Force was placed on alert to transport ten tonnes of anti-tank grenades in two DC-6 aircraft from Montijo Air Base in Portugal to Goa to assist in its defence. When the Portuguese Air Force was unable to obtain stopover facilities at any air base along the way because most countries, including Pakistan, denied passage of Portuguese military aircraft, the mission was passed to the Portuguese international civilian airline TAP, which offered a Lockheed Constellation (registration CS-TLA) on charter. However, when permission to transport weapons through Karachi was denied by the Pakistani government, the Constellation landed in Goa at 18:00 on 17 December with a consignment of half a dozen bags of sausages as food supplies instead of the intended grenades. In addition it transported a contingent of female paratroopers to assist in the evacuation of Portuguese civilians.[45]

The Portuguese air presence in Goa at the time of hostilities was thus limited to the presence of two civilian transport aircraft, the Lockheed Constellation belonging to TAP and a Douglas DC-4 Skymaster belonging to the Goan airline Portuguese India Airlines. The Indians claimed that the Portuguese had a squadron of F-86 Sabres stationed at

Dabolim Airport—which later turned out to be false intelligence. Air defence was limited to a few obsolete anti-aircraft guns manned by two artillery units who had been smuggled into Goa disguised as footballteams.[31]

## *Portuguese civilian evacuation*

The military buildup created panic amongst Europeans in Goa, who were desperate to evacuate their families before the commencement of hostilities. On 9 December, the vessel *India* arrived at Goa's Mormugãoport en route to Lisbonfrom Timor. Despite orders from the Portuguese government in Lisbon not to allow anyone to embark on this vessel, Governor General Manuel Vassalo e Silva allowed 700 Portuguese civilians of European origin to board the ship and flee Goa. The ship had capacity for only 380 passengers, and was filled to its limits, with evacuees occupying even the toilets.[31]On arranging this evacuation of women and children, Vassalo e Silva remarked to the press, "If necessary, we will die here." Evacuation of European civilians continued by air even after the commencement of Indian air strikes.[46]

## *Indian reconnaissance operations*

Indian reconnaissanceoperations had commenced on 1 December, when two Leopard class frigates, the INS *Betwa* and the INS *Beas*, undertook linear patrolling of the Goa coast at a distance of 8 miles (13 km). By 8 December, the Indian Air Forcehad commenced baiting missions and fly-bys to lure out Portuguese air defences and fighters.[citation needed]

On 17 December, a tactical reconnaissance flight conducted by Squadron Leader I. S. Loughran in a <u>Vampire NF54 Night Fighter</u>over Dabolim Airport in Goa was met with five rounds fired from a ground anti-aircraft gun. The aircraft took evasive action by drastically dropping altitude and escaping out to sea. The anti-aircraft gun was later recovered near the <u>ATC building</u>with a round jammed in its breech.[47]

The Indian light aircraft carrier <u>INS Vikrant</u>was deployed 75 miles (121 km) off the coast of Goa to head a possible amphibious operation on Goa, as well as to deter any foreign military intervention.

## Commencement of hostilities

## Military actions in Goa

### Ground attack on Goa: North and North East sectors

This section **needs additional citations for verification**. Please help <u>improve this article</u>by <u>adding citations to reliable sources</u>. Unsourced material may be challenged and removed.

*Find sources:* <u>"Annexation of Goa"</u>– <u>news</u>·<u>newspapers</u>·<u>books</u>·<u>scholar</u>·<u>JSTOR</u>*(May 2018) (<u>Learn how and when to remove this template message</u>)*

On 11 December 1961, <u>17th Infantry Division</u>and attached troops of the Indian Army were ordered to advance into Goa to capture Panaji and Mormugão. The main thrust on Panaji was to be made by the <u>50th Para Brigade Group</u>, led by Brigadier <u>Sagat Singh</u>from the north. Another thrust was to be carried out by <u>63rd Indian Infantry Brigade</u>from the east. A <u>deceptive thrust</u>, in company strength, was to be made from the south along the Majali-Canacona-Margao axis.[48]

Although the 50th Para Brigade was charged with merely assisting the main thrust conducted by the 17th Infantry, its units moved rapidly across minefields, roadblocks and four riverine obstacles to be the first to reach Panaji.[49]

Hostilities at Goa began at 09:45 on 17 December 1961, when a unit of Indian troops attacked and occupied the town of Maulinguém in the north east, killing two Portuguese soldiers. The Portuguese 2nd EREC (*esquadrão de reconhecimento*—reconnaissancesquadron), stationed near Maulinguém, asked for permission to engage the Indians, but permission was refused at about 13:45.[50]During the afternoon of the 17th, the Portuguese command issued instructions that all orders to defending troops would be issued directly by headquarters, bypassing the local command outposts. This led to confusion in the chain of command.[50]At 02:00 on 18 December, the 2nd EREC was sent to the town of Doromagogo to support the withdrawal of police forces present in the area, and were attacked by Indian Army units on their return journey.[50]

At 04:00, the Indian assault commenced with artillery bombardment on Portuguese positions south of Maulinguém, launched on the basis of the false intelligence that the Portuguese had stationed heavy battle tanksin the area. By 04:30, Bicholim was under fire. At 04:40, the Portuguese forces destroyed the bridge at Bicholim and followed this with the destruction of the bridges at Chapora in Colvale and at Assonora at 05:00.[50]

On the morning of 18 December, the 50th Para Brigade of the Indian Army moved into Goa in three columns.

1. The eastern column comprised the 2<sup>nd</sup> Para Marathaadvanced towards the town of Pondain central Goa via Usgão.
2. The central column consisting of the 1<sup>st</sup> Para Punjabadvanced towards Panaji via the village of Banastari.
3. The western column—the main thrust of the attack—comprised the 2<sup>nd</sup> Sikh Light Infantryas well as an armoured division which crossed the border at 06:30 and advanced on Tivim.[48]

At 05:30, Portuguese troops left their barracks at Ponda in central Goa and marched towards the town of Usgão, in the direction of the advancing eastern column of the Indian 2<sup>nd</sup> Para Maratha, which was under the command of Major Dalip Singh Jind and included tanks of the Indian 7<sup>th</sup> Cavalry. At 09:00, these Portuguese troops reported that Indian troops had already covered half the distance to the town of Ponda.[50]

**Air raids over Goa**

A Canberra PR.9 taking off. The Indian Air Force used 20 small and lightweight Canberra bombers.

The first Indian raid was led by Wing Commander N.B. Menon on 18 December on the Dabolim Airport using 12 English Electric Canberraaircraft. 63,000 pounds of explosives were dropped within minutes, completely destroying the runway. In line with the mandate given by the Air Command, structures and facilities at the airfield were left undamaged.[34]

The second Indian raid was conducted on the same target by eight Canberras led by Wing Commander Surinder Singh, again leaving the airport's terminal and other buildings untouched. Two civilian transport aircraft—a Lockheed Constellationbelonging to the Portuguese airline TAP and a Douglas DC-4belonging to the Goan airline TAIP—were parked on the apron. On the night of 18 December, the Portuguese used both aircraft to evacuate the families of some government and military officials after airport workers had hastily recovered part of the heavily damaged runway that evening. The first aircraft to leave was the TAP Constellation, commanded by Manuel Correia Reis, which took off using only 700 metres; debris from the runway damaged the fuselage, causing 25 holes and a flat tire. To make the 'short take-off' possible, the pilots had jettisoned all the extra seats and other unwanted equipment.[52]The TAIP DC-4 then also took off, piloted by TAIP Director Major Solano de Almeida. The two aircraft successfully used the cover of night and very low altitudes to break through Indian aerial patrols and escape to Karachi, Pakistan.[53]

A third Indian raid was carried out by six Hawker Hunters, successfully targeting the wireless station at Bambolim with rockets and gun cannons.

The mandate to support ground troops was served by the de Havilland Vampiresof No. 45 squadron, which patrolled the sector but did not receive any requests into action. In an incident of friendly fire, two Vampires fired rockets into the positions of the 2nd Sikh Light Infantry, injuring two soldiers, while elsewhere, Indian ground troops mistakenly opened fire on an IAF T-6 Texan, causing minimal damage.

In later years, commentators have maintained that India's intense air strikes against the airfields were uncalled-for, since none of the targeted airports had any military capabilities and they did not cater to any military aircraft. As such, the airfields were defenceless civilian targets.[53]The Indian navy continues to control the Dabolim Airport, although it is also once more used as a civilian airport.

### Storming of Anjidiv Island[edit]

Description:
https://upload.wikimedia.org/
wikipedia/
en/
thumb/
9/99/
Question_book-new.svg/
50px-Question_book-new.svg.png

This section **does not** cite any sources. Please help improve this sectionby adding citations to reliable sources. Unsourced material may be challenged and removed. *(May 2018) (Learn how and when to remove this template message)*

Anjidivwas a small 1.5 km island of Portuguese India, then almost uninhabited, belonging to the District of Goa, although off the coast of the Indian state of Karnataka. On the island stood the ancient Anjidiv Fort, defended by a platoon of Goan soldiers of the Portuguese Army.

The Indian Naval Command assigned the task of securing Anjidiv to the cruiser INS *Mysore*and the frigate INS *Trishul*. Under covering artillery fire from the ships, Indian marinesunder the command of Lieutenant Arun Auditto stormed the island at 14:25 on 18 December and engaged the Portuguese garrison. The assault was repulsed by the Portuguese defenders, with seven Indian marines killed and 19 wounded. Among the Indian casualties were two officers.

The Portuguese defences were eventually overrun after fierce shelling from the Indian ships offshore. The island was secured by the Indians at 14:00 on the next day, all the Portuguese defenders being captured with the exception of two corporalsand one private. Hidden in the rocks, one corporal surrendered on 19 December. The other was captured in the afternoon of 20 December, but not before launching hand grenades that injured several Indian marines. The last of the three, Goan private Manuel Caetano, became the last Portuguese soldier in India to be captured, on 22 December, after he had reached the Indian shore by swimming.

### Naval battle at Mormugão harbour[edit]

Description:
https://upload.wikimedia.org/
wikipedia/commons/thumb/7/7f/
NRP_Afonso_de_Albuquerque.jpg/
220px-NRP_Afonso_de_Albuquerque.jpg

The NRP *Afonso de Albuquerque*

On the morning of 18 December, the Portuguese sloop NRP *Afonso de Albuquerque*was anchored off Mormugão Harbour. Besides engaging Indian naval units, the ship was also tasked with providing a coastal artillery battery to defend the harbour and adjoining beaches, and providing vital radio communications with Lisbon after on-shore radio facilities had been destroyed in Indian airstrikes.

At 09:00, three Indian frigates led by the INS *Betwa* took up position off the harbour, awaiting orders to attack the *Afonso* and secure sea access to the port. At 11:00, Indian planes bombed Mormugão harbour.[3]At 12:00, upon receiving clearance, the INS *Betwa* and the INS *Beas* entered the harbour and fired on the *Afonso* with their 4.5-inch guns while transmitting requests to surrender in morse codebetween shots. In response, the *Afonso* lifted anchor, headed out towards the enemy and returned fire with its 120 mm guns.

The *Afonso* was outnumbered by the Indians, and was at a severe disadvantage since it was in a confined position that restricted its manoeuvring, and because its four 120 mm guns could fire only two rounds a minute, as compared to the 16 rounds per minute of the guns aboard the Indian frigates. A few minutes into the exchange of fire, at 12:15, the *Afonso* took a direct hit in its control tower, injuring its weapons officer. At 12:25, an anti-personnel shrapnel bomb fired from an Indian vessel exploded directly over the ship, killing its radio officer and severely injuring its commander, Captain António da Cunha Aragão, after which First Officer Pinto da Cruz took command of the vessel. The ship's propulsion system was also badly damaged in this attack.

At 12:35, the *Afonso* swerved 180 degrees and was run aground against Bambolim beach. At that time, against the commander's orders, a white flagwas hoisted under instructions from the sergeant in charge of signals, but the flag coiled itself around the mast and as a result was not spotted by the Indians, who continued their barrage. The flag was immediately lowered.

Eventually at 12:50, after the *Afonso* had fired nearly 400 rounds at the Indians, hitting two of the Indian vessels, and had taken severe damage, the order was given to start abandoning ship. Under heavy fire directed at both the ship and the coast, non-essential crew including weapons staff left the ship and went ashore. They were followed at 13:10 by the rest of the crew, who, along with their injured commander, set fire to the ship and disembarked directly onto the beach. Following this, the commander was transferred by car to the hospital at Panaji. The NRP *Afonso de Albuquerque* lost 5 dead and 13 wounded in the battle.[3]

The sloop's crew formally surrendered with the remaining Portuguese forces on 19 December 1961 at 20:30.[15]As a gesture of goodwill, the commanders of the INS *Betwa* and the INS *Beas* later visited Captain Aragão as he lay recuperating in bed in Panaji.

The *Afonso*—having been renamed *Saravastri* by the Indian Navy—lay grounded at the beach near Dona Paula until 1962, when it was towed to Bombay and sold for scrap. Parts of the ship were recovered and are on display at the Naval Museum in Bombay.[3]

The Portuguese patrol boat NRP *Sirius*, under the command of Lieutenant Marques Silva, was also present at Goa. After observing *Afonso* running aground and not having communications from the Goa Naval Command, Lieutenant Marques Silva decided to scuttle the *Sirius*. This was done by damaging the propellers and making the boat hit the rocks. The eight men of the *Sirius*'s crew avoided being captured by the Indian forces and boarded a Greek freighter on which they reached Pakistan.

## Military actions in Daman

### Ground attack on Daman

Daman, approximately 72 km²in area, is at the south end of Gujaratbordering Maharashtra, approximately 193 km north of Bombay. The countryside is broken and interspersed with marsh, salt pans, streams, paddy fields, coconut and palm groves. The river Daman Ganga splits the capital city of Daman(Damão in Portuguese) into halves—Nani Daman (*Damão Pequeno*) and Moti Daman (*Damão Grande*). The strategically important features were Daman Fort (fortress of São Jerónimo) and the air control tower of Daman Airport.[54]

The Portuguese garrison in Daman was headed by Major António José da Costa Pinto (combining the roles of District Governor and military commander), with 360 soldiers of the Portuguese Army, 200 policemen and about

30 customs officials under him. The army forces consisted of two companies of _caçadores_(light infantry) and an artillery battery, organised as the battlegroup "Constantino de Bragança". The artillery battery was armed with 87.6 mm guns, but these had insufficient and old ammunition. The Portuguese also placed a 20 mm anti-aircraft gun ten days before the invasion to protect the artillery. Daman had been secured with small minefields and defensive shelters had been built.[41]

The advance on the enclave of Daman was conducted by the 1st Maratha Light Infantry Battalionunder the command of Lieutenant-Colonel S.J.S. Bhonsle[54]in a pre-dawn operation on 18 December.[48]The plan was to capture Daman piecemeal in four phases, starting with the area of the airfield, then progressively the open countryside, Damão Pequeno and finally Damão Grande including the fort.[54]

The advance commenced at 04:00 when one battalion and three companies of Indian soldiers progressed through the central area of the northern territory, aiming to seize the airfield.[41]However, the surprise was lost when the Indian A Company tried to capture the control tower and suffered three casualties. The Portuguese lost one soldier dead and six taken captive. The Indian D Company captured a position named "Point 365" just before the next morning. At the crack of dawn, two sorties by Indian Air Force Mystèrefighters struck Portuguese mortarpositions and guns inside Moti Daman Fort.[54]

At 04:30, the Indian artillery began to bombard Damão Grande. The artillery attack and transportation difficulties isolated the Portuguese command post there from the forces in Damão Pequeno. At 07:30, a Portuguese unit at the fortress of São Jerónimo fired mortars on Indian forces attempting to capture the airstrip.[41]

At 11:30, Portuguese forces resisting an Indian advance on the eastern border at Varacunda ran out of ammunition and withdrew westwards to Catra. At 12:00, to delay the Indian advance following the withdrawal from Varacunda, the Portuguese artillery battery on the banks of the Rio Sandalcalo was ordered to open fire. The commander of the battery, Captain Felgueiras de Sousa, instead dismantled the guns and surrendered to the Indians.[41]By 12:00, the airfield was assaulted by the Indian A and C companies simultaneously. In the ensuing exchange of fire the A Company lost one more soldier and seven were wounded.[54]

By 13:00, the remaining Portuguese forces on the east border at Calicachigão exhausted their ammunition and retreated towards the coast. By 17:00, in the absence of resistance, the Indians had managed to occupy most of the territory, except the airfield and Damão Pequeno, where the Portuguese were making their last stand. By this time, the Indian Air Force had conducted six air attacks, severely demoralising the Portuguese forces. At 20:00, after a meeting between the Portuguese commanders, a delegation was dispatched to the Indian lines to open negotiations, but was fired on, and was forced to withdraw. A similar attempt by the artillery to surrender at 08:00 next day was also fired on.[41]

The Indians assaulted the airfield the next morning, upon which the Portuguese surrendered at 11:00 without a fight.[48]Garrison commander Major Costa Pinto, although wounded, was stretchered to the airfield, as the Indians were only willing to accept a surrender from him.[41]Approximately 600 Portuguese soldiers and policemen (including 24 officers[54]) were taken prisoner.

The Indians suffered 4 dead and 14 wounded,[54] while the Portuguese suffered 10 dead and two wounded.[48] The 1st Light Maratha Infantry was decorated for the battle with one VSM for the commanding officer, two Sena Medals and five Mentioned in Dispatches.[54]

### Daman air raids

In the Daman sector, Indian Mystères flew 14 sorties, continuously harassing Portuguese artillery positions.

### Naval action at Daman[edit]

Description:

https://upload.wikimedia.org/wikipedia/en/thumb/9/99/Question_book-new.svg/50px-Question_book-new.svg.png

This section **does not** cite any sources. Please help improve this section by adding citations to reliable sources. Unsourced material may be challenged and removed. (*May 2018*) (*Learn how and when to remove this template message*)

Like the *Vega* in Diu, the patrol boat NRP *Antares*—based at Daman under the command of 2nd Lieutenant Abreu Brito—was ordered to sail out and fight the imminent Indian invasion. The boat stayed in position from 07:00 on 18 December and remained a mute witness to repeated air strikes followed by ground invasion until 19:20, when it lost all communications with land.

With all information pointing to total occupation of all Portuguese enclaves in India, Lieutenant Brito decided to save his crew and vessel by escaping; the *Vega* traversed 530 miles (850 km), escaping detection by Indian forces, and arrived at Karachi at 20:00 on 20 December.

## Military actions in Diu

### Ground attack on Diu

Diu is a 13.8 km by 4.6 km island (area about 40 km$^2$) at the south tip of Gujarat. The island is separated from the mainland by a narrow channel running through a swamp. The channel could only be used by fishing boats and small craft. No bridges crossed the channels at the time of hostilities. The Portuguese garrison in Diu was headed by Major Fernando de Almeida e Vasconcelos (district governor and military commander), with around 400 soldiers and police officers, organised as the battlegroup "António da Silveira".[55]

Diu was attacked on 18 December from the north west along Kob Forte by two companies of the 20th Rajput Battalion—with the capture of the Diu Airfield being the primary objective—and from the northeast along Gogal and Amdepur by the Rajput B Company and the 4th Madras Battalion.[48]

These Indian Army units ignored requests from Wing Commander M.P.O. "Micky" Blake, planning-in-charge of the Indian Air Force operations in Diu, to attack only on first light when close air support would be available.[55] The Portuguese defences repulsed the attack backed by 87.6mm artillery and mortars,[41] inflicting heavy losses on the Indians.[55] The first attack was made by the 4th Madras on a police border post at 01:30 on 18 December at Gogol and was repulsed by 13 Portuguese police officers.[41] Another attempt by the 4th Madras at 02:00 was again repulsed, this time backed with Portuguese 87.5mm artillery and mortar which suffered due to poor quality of munitions. By 04:00, ten of the original 13 Portuguese defenders at Gogol had been wounded and were evacuated to a hospital. At 05:30, the Portuguese artillery launched a fresh attack on the 4th Madras assaulting Gogol and forced their retreat.[41]

Meanwhile, at 03:00, two companies of the 20th Rajput attempted to cross a muddy swamp[41] separating them from the Portuguese forces at Passo Covo under cover of dark on rafts made of bamboo cots tied to oil barrels.[55] The attempt was to establish a bridgehead and capture the airfield.[48]

This attack was repulsed with fairly heavy losses by a well entrenched unit of Portuguese soldiers armed with small automatic weapons and Sten guns[55] as well as light and medium machine guns. According to Indian sources this unit included between 125 and 130 soldiers,[48] but according to Portuguese sources this post was defended by only eight soldiers.[41]

As the Rajputs reached the middle of the creek, the Portuguese on Diu opened fire with two medium and two light machine-guns, capsizing some of the rafts. Major Mal Singh of the Indian Army along with five men pressed on his advance and crossed the creek. On reaching the far bank, he and his men assaulted the light machine gun trenches at Fort-De-Cova and silenced them. The Portuguese medium machine gun fire from another position wounded the officer and two of his men. However, with the efforts of company Havildar Major Mohan Singh and two other men, the three wounded were evacuated back across the creek to safety. As dawn approached, the Portuguese increased the intensity of fire and the battalion's water crossing equipment suffered extensive damage. As a result, the Indian battalion was ordered to fall back to Kob village by first light.[54]

Another assault at 05:00 was similarly repulsed by the Portuguese defenders. At 06:30, Portuguese forces retrieved rafts abandoned by the 20th Rajput, recovered ammunition left behind and rescued a wounded Indian soldier, who was given treatment.[41]

At 07:00, with the onset of dawn, Indian air strikes began, forcing the Portuguese to retreat from Passo Covo to the town of Malala. By 09:00 the Portuguese unit at Gogol also retreated,[41]allowing the Rajput B Company (who replaced the 4th Madras) to advance under heavy artillery fire and occupy the town.[48]By 10:15, the Indian cruiser INS Delhi, anchored off Diu, began to bombard targets on the shore.[41]At 12:45, Indian jets fired a rocket at a mortar at Diu Fortresscausing a fire near a munitions dump, forcing the Portuguese to order the evacuation of the fortress—a task completed by 14:15 under heavy bombardment from the Indians.[41]

At 18:00, the Portuguese commanders agreed in a meeting that, in view of repeated air strikes and the inability to establish contact with headquarters in Goa or Lisbon, there was no way to pursue an effective defence and decided to surrender to the Indians.[41]On 19 December, by 12:00, the Portuguese formally surrendered. The Indians took 403 prisoners, which included the Governor of the island along with 18 officers and 43 sergeants.[54]

In surrendering to the Indians, the Diu Governor stated that he could have kept the Army out for a few weeks but he had no answer to the Air Force. The Indian Air Force was also present at the ceremony and was represented by Gp Capt Godkhindi, Wing Cmdr Micky Blake and Sqn Ldr Nobby Clarke.[55]7 Portuguese soldiers were killed in the battle.[55]

Major Mal Singh and Sepoy Hakam Singh of the Indian army were awarded Ashok Chakra (Class III).[54]

On 19 December, the 4th Madras C Company landed on the island of Panikotoff Diu, where a group of 13 Portuguese soldiers surrendered to them there.[48]